504

THE KING PENGUIN BOOKS

·◁ 65 ▷·

SEMI-PRECIOUS STONES

N. WOOSTER

SEMI-PRECIOUS STONES

WITH SIXTEEN COLOURED PLATES BY
ARTHUR SMITH

PENGUIN BOOKS

HARMONDSWORTH · MIDDLESEX

1952

THE KING PENGUIN BOOKS
EDITOR : N. B. L. PEVSNER · TECHNICAL EDITOR : R. B. FISHENDEN
PUBLISHED BY PENGUIN BOOKS LTD
HARMONDSWORTH, MIDDLESEX, ENGLAND
PENGUIN BOOKS INC, 3300 CLIPPER MILL ROAD, BALTIMORE 11
MARYLAND, U.S.A.
PENGUIN BOOKS PTY LTD, 200 NORMANBY ROAD
MELBOURNE, AUSTRALIA

FIRST PUBLISHED 1952

TEXT PAGES PRINTED BY
R. AND R. CLARK LTD, EDINBURGH
PLATES MADE AND PRINTED BY
JOHN SWAIN AND SONS LTD, BARNET
COVER DESIGNED BY ARTHUR SMITH
MADE IN GREAT BRITAIN

SEMI-PRECIOUS STONES

SINCE THE EARLIEST TIMES people have been attracted by the stones which are classed together as 'semi-precious'. They mostly lack the brilliance and fire of the so-called 'precious' stones, neither are they surrounded by the glamour of extreme rarity, but they compensate for this by an unostentatious charm and individuality. The great majority of semi-precious stones are minerals. A few come from animals or plants. Odontolites, which are sometimes mistaken for turquoise, come from fossil teeth and bones; mother-of-pearl is the lining of oyster shells; coral is the hard stony skeleton of colonies of small animals growing in shallow sea-water; jet is a specially hard kind of anthracite; and another semi-precious stone of vegetable origin is amber, a fossil resin.

Certain uses of semi-precious stones have disappeared in the course of time – for instance the manufacture of eyes for mummy-cases, which must have been quite an important industry in ancient Egypt, to judge by the numbers surviving to the present day. The finest of these are quite lifelike imitations of natural eyes. The white was made of alabaster or opaque white quartz. Into this a circular recess was ground to take the iris, a circular piece of transparent, polished, and colourless quartz, in which a hole was bored to represent the pupil. The iris was coloured by sticking it in place with a dark brown or nearly black resin, which was also used to fill the pupil.

Semi-precious stones are used for jewellery and as a raw material for seals, statuettes, and vases or bowls; for inlaying furniture or the walls of buildings, and even as a building material when extensive deposits are found. A sizeable find of selenite was made in Nero's time and quarried for building a mausoleum. Built entirely without windows, this was filled with a yellow light, because of the translucency of the material. Enormous deposits of malachite have been discovered in the Urals, and solid malachite pillars hold up the roof of a hall in the Winter Palace in Leningrad. An imaginative application of the great variety of semi-precious stones found in the U.S.S.R. is a huge wall map in the Hermitage at Leningrad. The lakes and rivers are made of lapis lazuli, the forests and mountains of green and brown jaspers, and so on.

The popularity of various stones has changed much with changes of fashion, though an exception to this statement is the permanent pre-eminence of jade in China, where for thousands of years it has been valued above all precious stones. Yellow stones were more fashionable than others in ancient Greece, and most of the best Greek intaglios were cut into yellow stones, but yellow was a despised colour among the Romans, green stones being their first favourites. Turquoise was always greatly admired in Egypt and Persia. During the Renaissance no European gentleman with any pretensions to fashion would have been seen without a turquoise ring. Though blue turquoise is the only kind to have any value today, the green sort was the more admired in the past. Pliny asserts that 'the best turquoise is that which approacheth nearest to the grasse green of an emeraud'. In Victorian times, after the death of the Prince Consort, jet became most fashionable, but it is very little in demand now.

With the exception of jade, which embraces two mineral species, each particular kind of semi-precious stone has, within certain well-defined limits, a definite chemical composition. But striking differences in colour may result from barely detectable amounts of foreign atoms. The properties of a stone do not depend, however, on its chemical composition alone. Of importance, too, is the regularity with which its constituent atoms are arranged. When this orderliness

6

is nearly perfect, a clear single crystal results. Where the stone is built up of myriads of tiny crystallites arranged more or less regularly, it is said to be cryptocrystalline. Such stones are commonly translucent. Where there is no detectable regularity it is said to be massive. Such stones are frequently opaque.

Because the main substance of a given species is constant it follows that, however different one specimen may look from others, they will all have substantially the same specific gravity and hardness, since both these properties are affected only slightly by small changes in chemical composition and the degree of regularity of arrangement. It is, therefore, on these two characters that the identification of a stone usually rests. In this connexion hardness is defined as resistance to scratching. It is measured in terms of an arbitrary scale designed by Mohs in 1822. He arranged ten minerals in order of increasing hardness and assigned a number to each: (1) talc, (2) gypsum, (3) calcite, (4) fluorspar, (5) apatite, (6) orthoclase, (7) quartz, (8) topaz, (9) corundum, (10) diamond. The mineral with the higher number could scratch the mineral below it, but could not be scratched by it. A mineral is said to have a hardness of $6\frac{1}{2}$, say, if it is scratched by quartz, and is able to scratch orthoclase.

These two criteria for identifying stones, specific gravity and hardness, were used at least as early as the eleventh century by Arab mineralogists and jewellers, but in the subsequent centuries this really scientific approach was forgotten and reliance was placed mainly upon the appearance of a stone. The result is that, while it is easy to understand what stone is being described in the twelfth-century manuscript of Mohammed ben Mansur, the identity of a stone described in the seventeenth century may be quite impossible to establish.

The choice of the stones included in this small book is arbitrary, preference being given to those with curious legends or those that lend themselves to providing interesting coloured plates. Where to draw the line between precious and semi-precious stones on the one hand, and between semi-precious and building stones on the other, is at best a matter of opinion and prejudice. Remembering the story of the man and the ass, I have made a selection that seemed good to me, and offer no other justification.

Stone Lore

The history of the lore of precious and semi-precious stones in Europe is a sad confirmation of Plato's cynical dictum that you can make people believe anything if only you try hard enough. The 'incredible fabulosities' attaching to stones were not myths that encrusted the stones from remote antiquity, but sedulously cultivated superstitions inculcated among the ordinary people by the decadent priesthoods of Greece and Rome. The priests were successful against the passionate opposition of rational natural historians like Epicurus and Lucretius. Pliny, who was one of the latter, wrote that he aimed to

advance the knowledge of posterity in those things that may profit this life, and I meane eftsoones to have a fling at Magicians for their abhominable lies and monstrous vanities, for in nothing so much have they overpassed themselves as in the reports of gems and pretious stones, exceeding the tearms and limits of Physick, whiles under color of faire and pleasing medicines they hold us with a tale of their prodigious effects and incredible.

But in spite of his efforts the peoples of his and succeeding generations were enslaved within the anti-scientific and irrational attitude which was at the same time the cause and the curse of the Dark Ages. They accepted the stories of the 'impudent Magi' and added their own, using stones in magical practices and as therapeutic agents without scepticism or criticism until well on into the Renaissance.

8

We are apt to take the present disregard in our country of the magical qualities of stones as evidence that our contemporaries behave more rationally than our ancestors. That this is unwarranted is shown by the present use of scarce newsprint for astrological predictions, the faith in patent medicines, and the crepuscular political prejudices that are common today. It is just a change in fashion.

That stones could breed stones was one of the more extraordinary beliefs that were countenanced. Quite a number of instances are recorded of pearls and stones put away in boxes 'breeding' more of their kind, which led to the corollary that some varieties of stone were male and others female. (It goes without saying that the male were those which exhibited the more intense and beautiful colours.)

In times when the Evil Eye was a power to be reckoned with, when diseases were regarded as punishments or ascribed to poison or malignant spirits, when not only hell, but much of the earth was peopled with devils, semi-precious stones were much in demand as amulets. Coral, malachite, and eye-onyxes – which are red-and-white or black-and-white sards in which the layers are arranged concentrically – were particularly efficacious against the Evil Eye. Every need had its appropriate charm. Heliotrope had the property of bringing clouds together and evoking tempests. In the translation of the *Polyhistor* of Solinus, published by Arthur Golding in 1587, we read:

THE HELYTROPE OR TURN STONE

It is of a green colour not altogether verye fresh, but somewhat more cloudie and deepe, powdered about with spots of scarlett. The stone taketh his name of hys operation and power. Beeing cast into a brasse panne it altereth the colour of the Sunne beames, making them to have a bloody reflexion: and it casteth the glymering brightness of the ayre out of the water and turneth it aside. Moreover it is reported to have this vertue, it beeing mingled wyth the herb of the same name, and consecrated before with accustomable enchantments, it maketh the bearer thereof to goe invisible.

Loadstone prevented brothers from quarrelling, haematite ensured the success of lawsuits, the fertility of a field was guaranteed if the ploughman tied a light-green jasper mottled with yellow to his arm. A vermilion-coloured jasper made athletes invincible, a legend which doubtless accounts for the large numbers of these stones engraved with the figure of Hercules strangling a lion; for the virtue of a stone was held to be enhanced by a suitable engraving.

Turquoise had the valuable and odd power of protecting its wearer should he sustain a fall. Numerous stories are told where a turquoise which was being worn at the time of an accident saved its owner from a fractured bone by itself becoming cracked. Turquoise also possessed the remarkable property of growing paler when its owner sickened, and then regaining its colour when placed on the finger of a healthy person. It could also be used for telling the time, for, suspended on a fine string inside a glass, it would strike the hour by hitting the sides the proper number of times. Solinus says:

The Pyrrhite is the colour of golde and wyll not suffer himselfe to bee helde over close in ones hande, for if it chaunce to be strayned over hard, it burneth the fingers.

I have tried this experiment, but have not succeeded in 'overstrayning' sufficiently to observe the effect. Having no goats available I have been unable to confirm or deny Heraclius (he prefaced his book by saying, 'I will write nothing that has not first been tested'), that pyrites could be used for engraving glass:

Collect fat earth-worms as turned up by the plough, vinegar, and the hot blood out of a big he-goat fed on strengthening herbs; mix all together and so anoint the bright shining bowl, and then engrave upon it with fragments of the hard stone called Pyrites.

Though Pliny made a sharp distinction between such claims and 'the faire and pleasing medicines' that could be obtained by their use, these supposed therapeutic virtues seem to us just as fantastic. There were two ways of administering stones – either they were powdered and swallowed or made into ointments for local application, or they might be efficacious simply by being worn. Even as late as 1609 red jaspers were being recommended in cases of haemorrhage. De Boot describes how he himself had seen effects that were scarcely credible, and mentions that it was widely held that if a green jasper were engraved with the figure of a scorpion while the sun was entering that House of the Zodiac, it would be a sure prophylactic against the formation of stone in the bladder.

De Boot also held in the highest esteem Jade as a cure for diseases of the kidney. As mentioned earlier, jade embraces two minerals, nephrite and jadeite. The one name comes from the Greek word for kidney, *nephros*, the other from the Spanish word *ijada* which means flank. De Boot describes some wonderful cases to prove the potent curative properties of jade, the method being merely to tie the stone to the arm. He found some of his patients were obliged to wear it perpetually, as they relapsed as soon as it was removed. Not unnaturally it was extremely expensive. The idea seems to have been imported with jade by the Spaniards from America. Jade was unknown to the Ancients.

In China jade was regarded as the most pure and most divine of natural substances, so that not only did it play an important role in occult ceremonies but became entwined with their whole civilization and life in a thousand ways. Astronomical instruments, sacrificial knives, and libation vessels were made of it. It was used in both the worship of Heaven and the cult of ancestors. Though jade was made into amulets (and everything else, for that matter, from coats of mail to bird-cages), the feeling towards it was not based so much on superstitions as on a sense of its symbolic powers, if one may judge from the following extract from the *Li Ki*, an ancient book of religious ritual:

Benevolence lies in its gleaming surface,
Knowledge in its luminous quality,
Uprightness in its unyieldingness,
Power in its harmlessness,
Purity of soul in its rarity and spotlessness,
Eternity in its durability,
Moral leadership in its going from hand to hand without being sullied.

Until recently, and perhaps even today, the Chinese have been wont to hold a piece of jade in their hand and rub it when they have something important to discuss. And the highest form of praise is to be likened to jade.

Powdered rock crystal was prescribed to be taken in a mixture of wine and honey to stimulate the milk flow in nursing mothers. It was also said to be an antidote to poison.

Jet was alleged to have extraordinary properties. The fumes of it when burning immediately induced a fit in anyone subject to epilepsy. The fumes were useful too in driving away reptiles. Water in which jet had been steeped was an infallible test of female chastity. Mixed with wine, powdered jet was good for toothache, and with beeswax it made a sovereign remedy for tumours. The Magi used it for a peculiar mode of divination called Axinomantia, for it would not burn if the wish of the consulting party was destined to be fulfilled.

Galen gave the weight of his authority to the curative value of certain stones, though he doubted whether engraving improved their value:

The Green Jasper benefits the chest and mouth of the Stomach if tied upon it. Some set it in a ring and engrave upon it a serpent with radiated head ... of this gem I have had ample experience, having made a neck-

lace out of such stones and hung it round the neck, descending so low that the stones might touch the mouth of the stomach, and they proved to be of no less value than if they had been engraved.

A number of plasmas have been found, engraved with the serpent Chnuphis, surrounded by a long Coptic legend, and in one an invocation in Greek 'that he would keep in health the chest of Proclus'.

Amber, being so different in many ways from other stones, excited a great deal of interest and was endowed with more than its fair share of wonderful properties. Its origin, too, was subject to much unbridled speculation. Pliny writes:

I think it not impertinent to deliver what marveiles and wonders the Greeks have broached as touching this thing, that the age and posterity ensuing may yet be acquainted with their fabulosities ... many of their Poets ... tell us a tale of the sisters of young prince Phaeton, who weeping piteously for the miserable death of their brother who was smitten with lightning, were turned into poplar trees, which instead of tears yeelded every yere a certain liquor called Electrum (id est Amber). ... But that this is one of their loud lies, it appears evidently by the testimony of all Italie. ... Those that write more modestly than the rest (and yet can lie as well as the best) bears us in hand that about the saides of the Adriatick sea, upon rocks otherwise inaccessible, there grow trees which yerely at the rising of the Dogstar do yeeld forth this Amber in the manner of a gum. Theophrastus contrariwise affirms that Amber is digged out of the ground. ... Demostratus cals Amber, Lyncurion, for that it commeth of the urine of the wild beast named Onces or Lynces: the which is distinct in colour, for that which proceedeth from the male is reddish and of a fiery colour; the other which passeth from the female, is more weak in colour, and enclineth rather to whitish. ... Pytheas affirmeth, that in Alamin there is ... an Island called Abalus, into which at every spring tide, there is cast up by the waters of the sea at high water a great quantitye of Amber; and it is taken for nothing else than a certain excrement congealed and hardned, which the sea in that season purgeth and sendeth away. The inhabitants of those parts (saith he) use it for their ordinary fuel to burn. ... But I wonder most at Sophocles the Tragicall Poet ... who sticketh not to avouch, that beyond India it proceedeth from the tears that fall from the eies of the birds Meleagrides, wailing and weeping for the death of Meleager. Who would not marvel that either himself should be of that belief or hope to persuade others to his opinion? ... What should a man say to this? But that any man should seriously and by way of history deliver such stuff ... is a mere mockery of the world in the highest degree; a contempt offered to all men, and argueth an habit of lying, and an impunitie of that vice intollerable. But to leave Poets with their tales ... knowne it is for certain that engendered it is in certain Islands of the Ocean Septentrional where it beateth upon the coasts of Germany, and the Almanes call it Glessum. ... It is engendered then in certain trees, resembling Pines in some sort, and issueth forth from the marrow of them like as gum in Cherrie trees, and rosin in Pines. And verily, these trees are so full of this liquor that it swelleth and breaketh forth in abundance which afterwards either congealeth with the cold or thickeneth with the heat of autumn.

Amber in Pliny's time was in demand not only for 'faire carkanets and collers of Amber beadds' but also for carving in bowls and small figures, which fetched high prices, so that Pliny was full of scorn for the senseless extravagance of his compatriots, but he continues:

And yet I will not disgrace Amber too much: for why? there is some good use thereof in Physicke. ... True it is that a collar of Ambre beads worn about the neck of yong infants, is a singular preservative to them against secret poyson and a counatercharm for witchcraft and sorcery. Callistratus saith, that such collars are very good for all ages, and namely to preserve as many as weare them against fantasticall illusions and frights that drive folke out of their wits: yea and Amber, whether it be taken in drinke, or hung about one, cures the difficulty of voiding urin

... that if it be worn about the neck in a collar it cures feuers, and healeth the diseases of the mouth, throat and jawes: reduced to powder and tempered with honey and oile of roses it is soveraign for the infirmities of the ears. Stamped together with the best Attick hony, it makes a singular eie-salve for to help a dim sight: pulverized and the pouder thereof taken simply alone, or els drunk in water with masticke, is soveraign for the maladies of the stomacke.

Although the belief in the curative powers of most stones has disappeared (and probably the power of doctors to treat hysteric diseases successfully at the same time), the belief in amber has persisted. In C. W. King's book there is a footnote at the end of the chapter on amber:

That the wearing of an amber necklace will keep off the attacks of erysipelas in a person subject to them has been proved by repeated experiment beyond all possibility of doubt. Its action here cannot be explained, but its efficacy as a defence against chills of the throat is evidently due to its extreme warmth when in contact with the skin and the circle of electricity so maintained.

A similar claim was seen in a shop in the nineteen-thirties, and may be there today. How far the shopkeeper believed in his advocacy I do not know; perhaps it was no more genuine than the priests' in Greece, who spread 'their intollerable lies' with an ulterior motive.

The ancient Gauls decorated their swords, shields, and helmets with coral and amber; these were their only jewels. In Pliny's time most of the coral dredged from the Mediterranean was exported to the Far East. Much went to India where the Brahmins used it in divination. In China it was popular for decorating the symbolic sword and sheath in use for marriage ceremonies in some places. In later times a sphere of coral weighing about an ounce was attached to the top of a mandarin's hat. In Europe during the Renaissance it was often carved into statuettes.

One of the names by which coral was known in the past was gorgonia, from the legend that it originated when the newly severed head of the Gorgon was put among the seaweed by Perseus.

Cutting and Polishing

Although it has often been said that the ancient Egyptians used emery to cut and polish their stones, careful investigation has not supported this contention, and it is more likely that quartz sand was used. Emery (corundum) was undoubtedly used, however, by the Assyrians from the earliest times for cutting their seals. At first they used it as a file, the idea of using the powder with a soft metal tool being a later development. The Greeks and Romans made use of deposits of emery found in the island of Naxos, but this was of inferior hardness to the Armenian stone, which was imported for use where expense was of secondary importance. Diamond chips were used in Pliny's time when they could be obtained, but they were extremely rare and expensive. If Pliny is to be believed, the method of dealing with diamonds destined to be so used was to soak the diamond in the warm blood of a billy-goat (as otherwise it was unbreakable), then hit it on an anvil with a hammer. The fragments were mounted in iron handles, and used as chisels to carve stones. Certainly some Roman glyptics do look as though they had been carved in this way.

That the Jews made use of emery is indicated by an interesting legend. It is said that Moses engraved the stones of the Rationale by means of a worm called Samir. The blood of this was so potent a menstruum that it would bite into any stone, however hard, leaving a hollow wherever it had touched. When the Temple was being built a supply of these worms was needed, but the secret of obtaining them had been lost. Solomon, with his usual acumen, devised a way out of this difficulty. He had some chicks taken from an ostrich nest, sealed up in a glass bottle and put within sight of the distracted mother bird. Finding herself unable to release the chicks, she flew off to the desert and returned with one of these worms with which she opened the bottle. This stratagem was then repeated as often as necessary. The Hebrew word for emery is Smyris.

The problem of shaping jade is in a category by itself. It is not that jade is particularly hard, but it is of an unexampled toughness. To carve jade is consequently an exceedingly slow process. Stone-age tools made from jade have been found in many parts of the world, Europe, Mexico, and New Zealand among others, but pre-eminently in China. It is not without its social significance that there is no historical tradition in Europe for fashioning jade into things of use and beauty. The elaborate and intricate designs that have been carved in China in this most intractable material are monuments not only to the skill and taste and patience of the carver (though this last is remarkable enough since the abrasive used was probably quartz sand); it betokens another attitude to life. It is doubtful whether jade is being carved in China today.

Alabaster and Selenite

Alabaster is the massive form of the mineral gypsum, hydrated calcium sulphate. It is a soft material, hardness 2 on Mohs' scale, and the specific gravity is about 2·3. It is often snow-white, but it may be traversed by coloured veins, or be itself coloured. Its softness and the fact that it takes a good polish invite its use as a material for carving. Because it is translucent it is also popular for light fittings.

Alabaster was widely used in ancient Egypt, both as a building material and as a raw material for *objets d'art*. There are many alabaster perfume jars, and it is from them that alabaster takes its present name (the Latin word for a perfume jar being *alabaster*). The stone was carved into jars with long necks which were easy to seal. When the oil was required the neck was broken. Casteline near Leghorn, Michigan and Tennessee are places where this mineral is quarried today.

When gypsum occurs in single crystals it is known as selenite. Very large crystals, up to five feet long, have been reported, often in extensive deposits. Selenite cleaves readily into thin diamond-shaped sheets – as Francis Willughby wrote in 1664: 'There is a kind of selenites ... which naturally roches into parallelipipedums of the figure of a lozenge.' When window glass was expensive these pieces were used for glazing, and it is very probable that diamond-leaded windows owe their origin to this. Selenite was used in this way in Roman Spain and Italy, and to this day there are old selenite windows in churches in Nicosia and Famagusta.

Amber

Amber is very different from all the other semi-precious stones, being the fossilized resin exuded by long-extinct coniferous trees. Sometimes insects or plants are found embedded in it, having got trapped while it was still fluid. It is an amorphous solid which feels very light and pleasantly warm to the touch. The colour varies from black to almost colourless, through all shades of brown, orange, and yellow. Rarely white, grey, greenish, bluish, or clear red specimens are found. The lustre is soft. Some pieces are quite transparent, others are opalescent, others again translucent, and some are quite opaque, looking like ivory. The opacity is due to minute air bubbles.

Though brittle it can be easily turned on a lathe. Most specimens take a good polish. The hardness is 2 to $2\frac{1}{2}$, which means that though it cannot be scratched with a finger-nail, it is easily marked with a knife. The specific gravity is 1 to 1·1, so that it will float on brine.

Amber is an extremely good electrical insulator. When rubbed it becomes electrically charged and will attract small fragments of metal, paper, straw, and the like. This property was known to the Ancients, and it was this characteristic that led to the word electricity, from the Greek name for amber – elektron. Our word amber comes from the Arabian word *anbar* which means ambergris, the waxy substance obtained from sperm whales. This looks rather like grey amber.

Most amber is obtained from the South Baltic coast near Königsberg (now Kaliningrad). It is also obtained from Sicily and Rumania, but the quality is not so good. It is sometimes to be picked up on the Norfolk coast after a storm. It is the only jewel mentioned in the *Iliad*.

Coral

Coral is the hard skeleton of a polyp which grows in warm shallow seas. It is found in many colours, but 'coral' pink and a kind of lacquer red are most sought after. It is a form of calcium carbonate, and the colours are due to organic pigments. The hardness is $3\frac{1}{2}$ and the specific gravity 2·6 to 2·7. It can be turned on a lathe and takes a good polish.

The word coral comes from a similar Greek word.

Coral is most abundant in the shallow parts of the Pacific Ocean where it has formed whole islands and the Great Barrier Reef. Plate 16 shows a coral, *coralium nobile* var., showing the pits for the polypes. Where this specimen was found is not recorded.

Fluorspar

Fluorspar, which is calcium fluoride, rivals quartz in the variety of colours it can exhibit and also in the size and perfection of some of the single crystals that are found. But it lacks the brilliant lustre characteristic of the silica minerals, and it is relatively soft; hence it is of no use as a gemstone. The fibrous kinds make beautiful bowls and vases.

The single crystals are usually found in the form of cubes. Some of them show a most interesting sort of twinning as though two cubes had interpenetrated each other with a diagonal in common (Plates 14 and 15). Fluorspar has a perfect cleavage, so that it is easy to transform a cube into an octahedron by knocking off the corners. Some naturally occurring octahedra are shown in Plate 1. The hardness is 4, the specific gravity 3·0 to 3·2. Many fluorspar crystals glow, sometimes for a long time, after exposure to light. This phenomenon is called phosphorescence. Other fluorspars have the property of emitting light of a certain wavelength if irradiated with light of a shorter wavelength. This is known as fluorescence, the name being derived from the fact that the phenomenon was discovered in fluorspar. The name fluorspar itself comes from *fluere* = flow, as it is easily fusible and is used as a flux in many metallurgical processes.

Though it is found in many places, the finest fluorspar is English. Bowls made from Derbyshire 'Bluejohn' were sought after by connoisseurs even in Roman times. A typical specimen is shown in Plate 15. Other fine deposits are found in Durham, Cumberland, and Cornwall, where it occurs in veins and pegmatites. Plate 13 shows a purple fluorspar from Weardale, Co. Durham, and Plate 14 a purple fluorspar associated with calcite on dolomite and haematite from Ullcoats Mine, Cumberland. A fluorspar associated with a pale yellow quartz and chalcopyrite is shown in Plate 1. This specimen was held against the light while it was drawn.

Iron Pyrites

This mineral is a sulphide of iron, and is a pale brassy yellow with a brilliant metallic lustre. Small crystals are sometimes used to provide a cheap substitute for diamonds, as numbers of them set close together provide a flashing and reasonably durable surface. It is interesting that when they are arranged in this way the yellowish colour is somehow disguised, and one gets the impression of a steel colour instead. The hardness is 6 to $6\frac{1}{2}$, the specific gravity 4·9 to 5·2. Most pyrites for decorative purposes is sold under the name marcasite, which is another form of the same chemical compound. (Marcasite, however, is less stable than pyrites, and tarnishes readily.) A fine group of iron pyrites crystals is shown in Plate 12.

Jade

Under the name Jade two distinct substances are included: jadeite, which is sodium aluminium silicate, and nephrite, which is calcium magnesium silicate. The ultimate arrangement of the atoms in these two minerals is very similar, and this gives rise to a striking similarity in most of their properties.

Jadeite is often granular in texture. It is harder ($6\frac{1}{2}$ to 7) than nephrite ($6\frac{1}{2}$) and has a higher specific gravity (3·3 to nephrite's 2·9 to 3·1). They are probably the toughest stones in existence and are consequently among the most difficult to work.

Jadeite may be brilliantly coloured – the greens are bright apple greens or emerald greens. The green of nephrite is greyish or brownish. But jade is not found only in shades of green or bluish-green. Many examples are brown or black, yellow, dazzling white, cream or white flecked with red. Rarely it is lacquer red or mottled purple. A mottled green boulder, weighing 134 lb, is shown in Plate 2. The apple-green colour in jadeite is due to the presence of chromium. This is never found in nephrites, their more sober greens being due to iron.

Jade is usually opaque or, at most, translucent, with a curious characteristic, almost greasy, lustre. But occasionally it is quite transparent. There is a beautiful collection of transparent jades, cut *en cabochon*, of all colours, in the London Chamber of Commerce Laboratory of Precious Stones.

Jade is found in river-beds and is also mined in quarries and underground mines. There used to be huge workings in Chinese Turkestan which have probably been exploited since the third millennium B.C. In 1764 it is recorded that 39 slabs weighing together 5300 lb were quarried there. But in the middle of the nineteenth century the Mohammedan population of Turkestan rose against the Chinese, and the quarries and mines fell into disuse.

The largest pieces of worked jade are probably a huge dark-green slab sealing the tomb of Tamerlane, and another great tombstone erected to a King of Annam. Among the most exquisite examples of Chinese art is a jade mountain scene nearly two feet high, which once occupied a place of honour in the Emperor's Summer Palace in Peking. Here are fir trees and bushes growing in crevices, clear streams, pavilions in sheltered nooks, and five poets 'drawing inspiration from Nature's own fount', the whole design miraculously hinged on the natural distribution of colour in the original boulder. Visitors to Milwaukee now have the privilege of admiring this work of art.

Jade is found in a great many places besides China and Burma, though these have been the main sources of the stone worked with such skill and delight by the Chinese. It is also found in Siberia, Alaska, Tibet, and New Zealand. Nephrite has been excavated in huge pieces in Jordanstal, Germany. A number of jade enthusiasts in the United States are looking for the stone in various likely localities in their country and have founded a society to further their interests.

Lapis Lazuli

Lapis Lazuli is a lovely blue stone, the Sapphirus of the Ancients. Unlike the majority of semi-precious stones it is not, as a rule, a substantially pure material. The bulk of most lapis is practically valueless; the colour for which it is prized is due to a small amount of an intense blue mineral, lazurite, which may constitute only a small proportion by weight. Lazurite is a sodium alumino-silicate, containing sulphur. The hardness is $5\frac{1}{2}$ to 5, the specific gravity $2\cdot4$. It is made synthetically now, and called ultramarine.

Lapis lazuli in the past was highly esteemed as a pigment for artists. It is used in this way today only for painting 'Old Masters'. Mostly it is valued as a raw material for jewellery, beads, buttons, for carving into statuettes or for inlay work or mosaics. It used to be a favourite material for seals and was often carved with royal portraits.

An even deep purplish blue 'like that of a dark-blue beetle' was regarded as the best colour in ancient days, better even than a royal blue 'spotted with gold dust', that is, spangled with iron pyrites. How attractive some of the less valued, mottled examples can be, is shown in Plate 3. This specimen is said to be Persian.

Lapis lazuli was used in Egypt from predynastic times. It was supposed to come from Persia, but in fact probably came from Badakhshan in north-east Afghanistan. The mines there were mentioned by Marco Polo. Persian merchants probably handled most of the trade. Lake Baikal in Siberia has produced some enormous pieces – vases carved from them in the Hermitage at Leningrad measure four feet across. Other countries of origin are Chile and California.

Malachite and Azurite

These two minerals are usually considered together as a pair, since they so commonly occur in the same specimen and are chemically much the same. Both are basic carbonates of copper. Azurite has a tendency to turn into the more stable form of malachite. The hardness of both minerals is $3\frac{1}{2}$, the specific gravity $3\cdot7$ to 4.

Malachite is usually massive and generally occurs as rounded nodules with a fibrous or banded structure, the colour inside varying from dark green through emerald and grass green to nearly white.

The patterns disclosed by cutting and polishing are sometimes quite fantastic and suggest all manner of things. Pliny called this mineral *smaragdus medicus*, 'found of greater dimensions than any other sort, of a wavy pattern representing poppies or birds' feathers, and sometimes resembling lapis lazuli'. Plate 10 shows some typical nodules from Park Downs Mine, Queensland.

Azurite may be massive, when it can vary from pale to deep azure blue, but it is often well crystallized, forming clusters of brilliant dark-blue crystals with an adamantine lustre. Plate 11 illustrates these two minerals associated with limonite. The specimen comes from the Copper Queen Mine, Bisbee, Arizona, U.S.A.

The name malachite is derived from *molochites*, a stone Pliny described, which was probably a green jasper.

Silica Minerals

Silica occurs in a great variety of forms and colours. In semi-precious stones it is crystallized in the form called quartz. The hardness is 7, or a little over in some varieties, the specific gravity 2·5 to 2·8, and the refractive index 1·54. Where single crystals occur, they are usually hexagonal prisms terminated at one end by a pyramid. The lustre is vitreous.

SINGLE-CRYSTAL VARIETIES

Reasonably good and sizeable crystals can be found in many parts of the world. In this country they are easy to find in veins in Cornwall and the Scottish Highlands. The best colourless crystals, and many beautifully coloured ones too, come from Brazil, where faultless crystals the size of footballs are not so uncommon, and crystals weighing tons have been found. Fine crystals have also been found in Madagascar, the Urals, the Swiss Alps, Japan, Arkansas, and other places too numerous to mention. Livia, wife of Augustus, dedicated a crystal weighing 150 lb in the Capitol.

Colourless quartz is known as rock crystal, and has been valued since very early times. Some examples are shown in Plate 1. In spite of its hardness it has been used for carving into bowls and vases. In classical times roughly fashioned bowls were imported from India to Alexandria, where they were finely wrought. Connoisseurs were prepared to pay extravagant prices for them.

The Greek word *krystallos* referred to both ice and quartz, for the latter was supposed to have been formed from ice that had been further congealed by intense cold. Three separate lines of evidence supported this theory – the best crystals the Greeks ever found occurred above the snow-line in the Alps, one sometimes came across crystals that contained liquid inclusions that looked like water, and hot liquids poured into rock-crystal vessels were liable to cause fracture. But this was not universally accepted. Solinus, who was probably a Roman jeweller and lived a little later than Pliny, wrote:

Some think the Ice congealeth and hardneth into Crystall, but this is false. For if it were so, neither Alaband of Asia nor the Isle of Cyprus should engender thys kind of stuffe, forasmuch as the heate in those countries is most vehement.

Traditionally crystal vessels were used only for serving cold liquids.

Because quartz has a high thermal conductivity it feels cool to the touch, and as a result crystal spheres were in great demand by Roman ladies to cool their hands. They were also used as burning glasses, and if a doctor wished to cauterize a wound, this was considered the instrument of choice. Such spheres are also the stock-in-trade of the crystal gazer. Quartz beads in modern times have been a quite important export from Germany and Japan.

Quartz coloured violet or purple is called Amethyst. This was originally imported into Greece from Persia, where its name was Shamest. Amethyst is clearly a corruption of this, but having once been given this name it was supposed to have been derived from two Greek words, a = without, and *methu* = alcohol. This gave rise to a belief that it was a specific against drunkenness, so that wine drunk from an amethyst bowl would not cause intoxication. This belief spread all over Europe and became current among the Arabs, and persisted for centuries. It suggests that amethyst drinking cups were very rare.

Indian amethysts, which were the colour of royal purple, were very valuable in Roman times. Indeed it is only quite recently that amethysts have become less expensive. A necklace 'of well-matched stones ' in the possession of Queen Charlotte in the eighteenth century was valued at two thousand pounds.

The colour of amethysts fades on heating, so that very dark stones which are apt to lack the brilliance of lighter ones are often heat-treated to improve their appearance. A very fine specimen from Brazil is shown in Plate 7.

Certain clear yellow quartzes of jewel quality are called Citrines. This was a favourite Greek stone, and many beautiful intaglios were cut in it. Pale stones were supposed to be female, and more intensely coloured ones male. Another name for citrine is false topaz, and it does resemble yellow topaz to some extent. The colour is due to a trace of ferric iron.

Another yellow or brown quartz is the Cairngorm, so called from being found in the Scottish Highlands. It differs from citrine in being 'smoky' in addition to its colour. The smokiness is the result of irradiation by radioactive minerals in the neighbourhood. It can be removed by heating, and simulated by exposure to X-rays. If the heating is carefully carried out yellow stones, very similar to citrines, can be produced. Cairngorms are usually brilliant cut, and are very popular in Scotland, particularly those that are whisky-coloured. Other localities famous for these stones are Pike's Peak, Colorado; Paris, Maine; the Alps; and Ceylon. They were also used in Ancient

Egypt as jewels, a deposit occurring at Romit in the Eastern Desert. The group shown in Plate 4 is from the St Gotthard.

Some yellow, brown, red, or green quartz crystals contain bright inclusions of mica or haematite which look like flakes of gold. These stones are called Aventurines, from a similarity they bear to a type of Venetian glass. As a result of a lucky accident (*per avventura*) a jar of brass filings was spilt into a vat of molten glass. The result was surprisingly attractive and called 'aventurine' glass. Pliny describes the natural stones, calling them *Coralloachates*, 'sprinkled with gold dust like lapis lazuli'.

There is also a rare dark-blue quartz crystal which is called Siderite. It is also known as sapphire quartz.

It is commonly believed that most varieties of coloured quartzes are to be found on the beaches in Cornwall. Encouraged by this tradition hundreds of visitors spend hours combing the seashore for likely looking pebbles, which the more optimistic take to a local lapidary for cutting and polishing. How well is their optimism justified! A few days later they receive in exchange for their drab stones (and the not inconsiderable fee for 'work done') beautiful clear, brightly coloured beads, all ready for threading on a 'necklace that I found myself'. It was not possible to get any stones cut and polished during the war, nor was it possible to import hundredweights of cheap Brazilian crystals, cut and polished and bored in Oberstein, Germany. This had been a regular feature of Cornish foreign trade in pre-war days. Perhaps now that trade is easier, the Cornish lapidaries have returned to work.

CRYPTOCRYSTALLINE VARIETIES

The proper nomenclature of the cryptocrystalline varieties and massive forms of silica is somewhat obscure. There are so many varieties and so many names that it is not very surprising if no two authorities seem to agree on the subject. The majority of the names today clearly derive from old Latin names, *e.g.* Chalcedony from Chalcedonius, Agate from Achates, Jasper from Jaspis, but unfortunately it is equally clear that the minerals Pliny was describing under these names are not the minerals to which we refer. Chalcedonius to Pliny was an inferior sort of emerald, a brilliant green, rather soft mineral, occurring as small crystals in the copper mines at Chalcedon. This is a hydrous copper silicate that we call Chrysocolla. In modern parlance Chalcedony refers to a cryptocrystalline variety of quartz, mostly semi-transparent or translucent, patchily coloured and either white, grey, yellowish, brown, or rarely blue. It may line cavities or occur as concretionary lumps or stalagmites, having crystallized out, in all probability, from masses of silica gel. In Roman times, when bowls were carved out of this material, they were said to be made of Murrhina. They were used to hold hot liquids.

Chalcedonies that are more brilliantly coloured are given special names. Chalcedony which is red and translucent is known as Sard or Common Carnelian. (The name sard came from Sardis in Lydia, not, as Theophrastrus suggested, because it was the colour of a pickled sardine.) Carnelian, which is a relatively modern name, comes from *carneus* = fleshy. If the stone is transparent, it is known as precious or oriental carnelian. This is a much rarer stone. A chalcedony which is white, flecked with red spots, is called St Stephen's Stone, and certain specimens have been venerated as relics of the martyrdom of St Stephen.

There is a number of green chalcedonies, coloured with traces of nickel, copper, or vanadium. Chrysoprase is apple green, prase leek green, plasma is dark green and usually contains white lines or patches, or has yellow or black spots. Heliotrope is a bright-green chalcedony containing bright red opaque spots. It should be distinguished from the Bloodstone, an opaque dark-green jasper with red spots, which is far commoner.

Achates was the name given by the Romans to a great variety of stones, because they were found in the river Achates in Sicily, but our agate is a chalcedony where the colours, which may be brilliant and varied, are distributed on a translucent ground in well-defined layers, often in more or less parallel lines or in concentric circles round a crystalline core. Plate 6 shows an agate from Uruguay, South America. Our moss- or tree-agate is a chalcedony which contains a dendritic distribution of colours caused by certain coloured impurities spreading out into the silica gel before solidification – not to the growth of the main body round some pre-existing dendritic inclusion. One known as a Mocha-stone is shown in Plate 5.

Onyx is a chalcedony showing straight parallel bands of black and white. In Sardonyx there is a similar arrangement of red and white bands. Formerly sardonyx was the name assigned to a three-fold sequence of red, white, and black. These banded stones are the raw material from which cameos are cut. Careful examination of some of the more skilful of these will show that traces of an uppermost layer have sometimes been utilized to enhance the interest of the carved figure, for instance where a suspicion of an upper layer of red has given a blush to a lady's cheek.

Nowadays opaque cryptocrystalline or massive quartzes are mostly known as jaspers. The famous Egyptian head of Nofretiti was carved in a yellow jasper. Sometimes jaspers contain white spots and lines. One, preserved in the Natural History Museum in London, is a convincing portrait of the poet Chaucer. Some rather fine blue jaspers of Persian origin are known.

Two other varieties of quartz deserve to be mentioned. One is Rose quartz, a delicate pink, translucent stone, which lends itself admirably to carving. The colour is due to a trace of manganese. The other is Tiger's Eye. This is a bright golden-yellow stone with a lively chatoyance. It is formed when a siliceous solution percolates between the fibres of a dark-blue asbestos called crocidolite. The colour of the asbestos is due to the large amount of ferrous iron it contains. When the solution seeps into the interstices between the fibres it reacts with them and oxidizes the iron to ferric oxide, and the whole mass changes into a quartz pseudomorph surrounding the remains of the asbestos fibres, which cause the chatoyance.

Turquoise

Turquoise is a basic phosphate of copper and aluminium with more or less iron in it. It may be sky blue, bluish-green, apple green, yellowish-green or grey-green in colour, the greenish tint being indicative of iron. It is the rarest experience to find it crystallized; usually it occurs as amorphous lumps, rounded pebbles, or as veins or disseminated grains in a limonite matrix. It is opaque except in the thinnest sections and has a peculiar waxy lustre. The hardness is 6 and the specific gravity between 2·6 and 2·8. The colour, which is usually much less attractive in artificial light than in sunlight, is liable to fade if exposed to strong light or heat. And because turquoise is somewhat porous, it is liable to absorb dirt and grease.

It has been used as a jewel from time immemorial. It was already being mined by the Egyptians in the fourth millennium B.C. Perhaps the most important turquoise mining locality in the world is between Nishapur and Meshbed in Persia, where it occurs in a weathered porphyry. Other important places are Sinai, Turkestan, New South Wales, Queensland, Victoria, Nevada, Arizona, New Mexico, and California.

The name means Turkish stone. The Persian name was *smaragdus*, the Egyptian *mafkat*. *Mafkat* was often wrongly translated as malachite, and Pliny's *smaragdus* is our malachite. Smaragdus is the name the Germans now give to the stone we call emerald. There is no better example of the confusion of names that occurs in this subject. But it is evidence, incidentally, that the green variety was more admired than the blue in other times than our own.

Two of the plates show turquoise – Plates 8 and 9. The former, a stone from Tibet, though an exceptionally fine specimen, is typical. The other, with its ravishing small nodules set in a black velvet cavity, is of the rarest, and comes from Liskeard, Cornwall. For many years it was lying in a museum labelled Henwoodite from Liskeard, Cornwall. I decided to promote henwoodite to be a semi-precious stone for the purposes of this book, but then doubt was cast upon whether it was henwoodite at all. So a small piece of one of the nodules, which are radiating crystals, was subjected to X-ray analysis, whereupon it was found to be genuine turquoise. After that all the henwoodite in the British Museum was examined and all of it was found to be turquoise.

ACKNOWLEDGEMENTS

The editor, artist, and author are indebted to Dr Campbell Smith, Keeper of Minerals at the British Museum (Natural History), for permission to make drawings of the specimens shown in Plates 1, 6, 11, 13, 14, 15, 16; to Dr J. Phemister, Director of the Geological Survey and Museum, London, for Plates 2, 3, 4, 5, 7, 9, 10, and 12; to Professor C. E. Tilley, F.R.S., of the Department of Mineralogy and Petrology, Cambridge University, for Plate 8; and to Mr C. H. Benson, of the Museum of Practical Geology, and Miss J. M. Sweet, of the British Museum (Natural History), for help given in the drawing of the plates. Dr F. A. Bannister at the British Museum kindly carried out an X-ray analysis of the Liskeard turquoise to establish its identity for us.

BIBLIOGRAPHY

ANSELME BOECE DE BOOT. *Le parfaict joaillier, ou histoire des pierreries.* Translated from the Latin by J. Bachou. Lyon, 1644.

CHARLES WILLIAM KING. *The Natural History, Ancient and Modern, of Precious Stones, Gems and Precious Metals.* London, 1865.

E. H. KRAUS AND C. B. SLAWSON. *Gems and Gem Materials.* McGraw-Hill, 1947.

G. F. KUNZ. *The Curious Lore of Precious Stones.* Philadelphia, 1913. *The Magic of Jewels and Charms.* Philadelphia, 1915.

MOHAMMED BEN MANSUR. *Book of Precious Stones.* Translated into German by von Hammer, 'Mines de l'Orient', vol. vi. 1818.

UNA POPE-HENNESSY. *Early Chinese Jades.* Benn, 1923.

PLINIUS SECUNDUS. *The Historie of the World.* Translated into English by Philemon Holland, 1634 (2nd edition).

GAIUS JULIUS SOLINUS. *Polyhistor.* Translated into English by A. Golding, 1587.

1. Fluorspar, Quartz, and Chalcopyrite

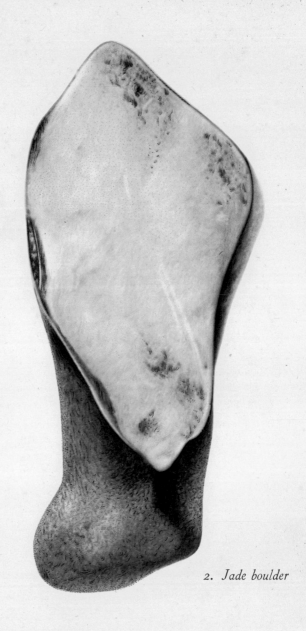

2. *Jade boulder*

3. *Lapis Lazuli*

4. *Quartz, variety Cairngorm*

5. *Quartz, variety Mocha Stone*

6. Quartz, variety Agate

7. Quartz, variety Amethyst

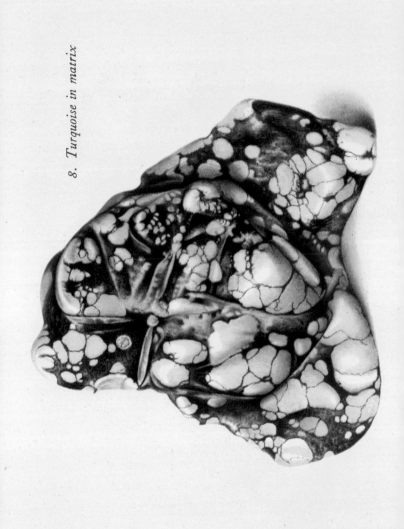

8. Turquoise in matrix

9. *Turquoise 'Henwoodite'*

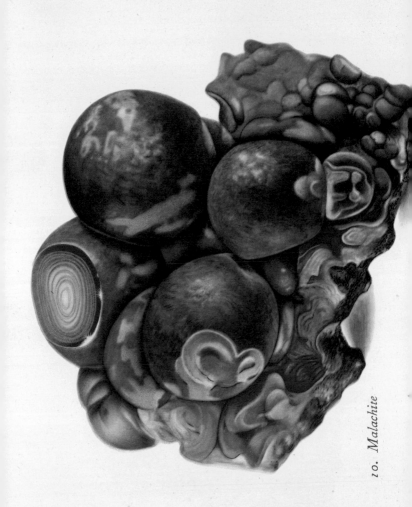

10. *Malachite*

11. *Azurite and Malachite*

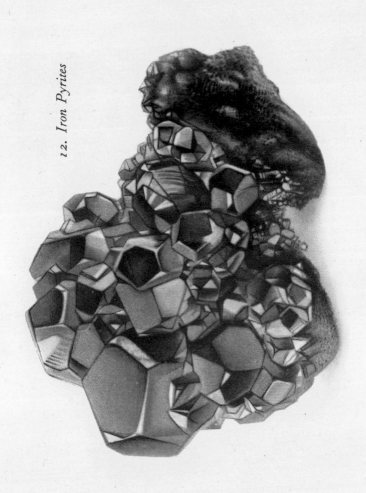

12. Iron Pyrites

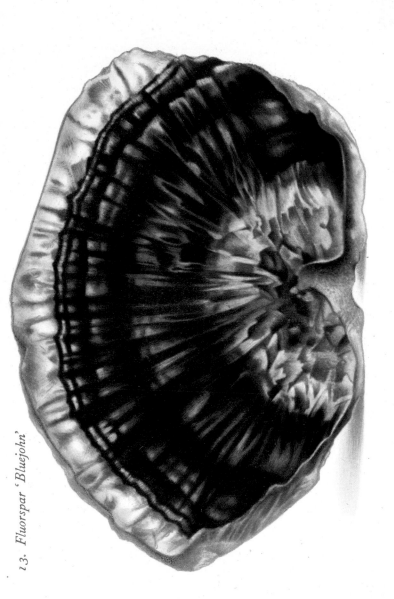

13. *Fluorspar 'Bluejohn'*

14. *Fluorspar*

15. Fluorspar

16. Coral